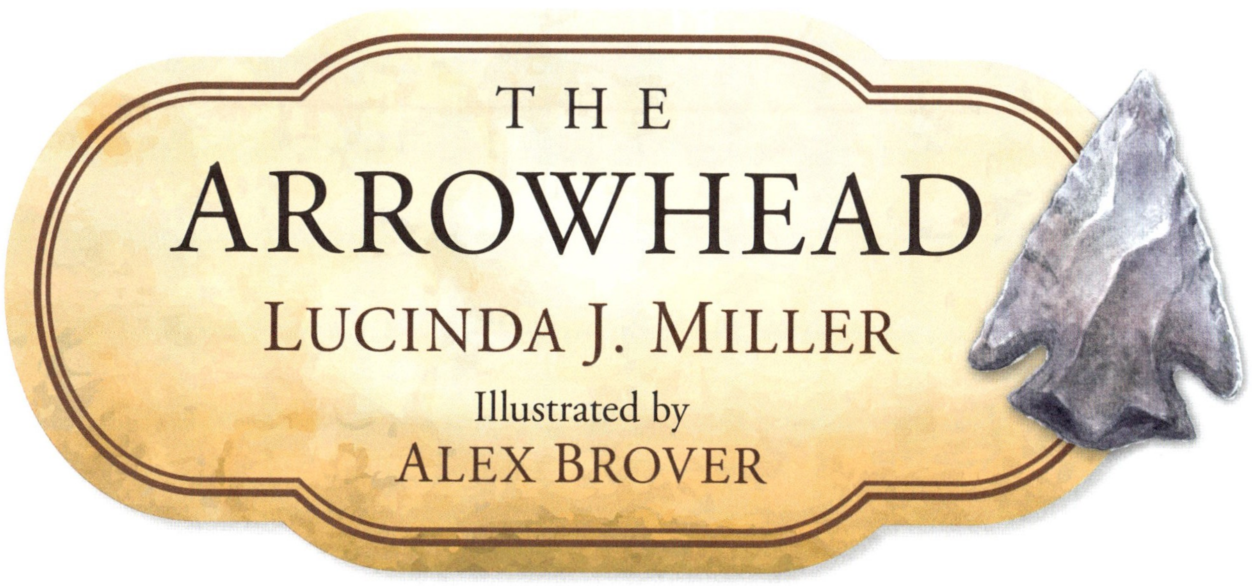


CHRISTIAN LIGHT PUBLICATIONS
*Harrisonburg, Virginia 22802*

THE ARROWHEAD
Christian Light Publications, Inc.
Harrisonburg, Virginia 22802


Illustrations: Alex Brover
Some illustrations based on the work of Sarah Douglass
and iStockphoto.com
Cover & Interior Design: David W. Miller

ISBN: 978-0-87813-273-7

# Dedication

*To Grandma Miller,*

*a praying woman*

# AUTHOR'S NOTE

When I was young, my dad told me the story of how, as a little boy, he prayed to find an arrowhead and how God answered his prayer. I wondered how many years that arrowhead had lain there before my grandfather's plow turned it up at just the right time, and I imagined a history for it. In this story, I picture my dad as the grandpa he now is, telling the story to one of his granddaughters.

*Tell me a story, Grandpa.*

Once, long ago,
an Indian shot at
a rabbit.

*Did he kill the rabbit?*

No, but he nicked the rabbit's foot with the wide stone arrowhead.

Pearls of blood fell,

droppity,

droppity,

drop, onto the ground.

But the rabbit ran,

hoppity, hoppity, hop, into a hole in the ground and escaped.

The arrowhead lay forgotten
on a pile of dirt that a
badger had made.

*What happened to the arrowhead?*

The sun shone on it.
The rain fell on it.

A deer stepped on it
and mashed it into the dirt.

An elm tree grew up beside the arrowhead, and it got tangled in a root.

*Did an Indian find the arrowhead one day?*

No. One day a family of white settlers moved in. They built a log cabin. They built a log fence and put a cow into it. They chopped down the tree where the arrowhead lay and used the ground as a field to grow corn for their cow.

*Did they find the arrowhead?*

No. The man and woman who built the log cabin and chopped down the tree grew old and died. Their son farmed the land. He built a new red barn and a white board house. He planted clover in the cornfield and used it as a pasture for his cows. Every day his little boy and his little girl walked out to the pasture with a big willow switch. They brought the cows in to the new red barn to be milked.

*Did the little boy and girl find the arrowhead?*

No. The little boy and girl grew up. The girl got married. The boy became a doctor. They sold the land to a skinny man with a ragged straw hat. The skinny man had a round wife and ten rowdy children. He planted potatoes in the clover field. Every fall he and his round wife and his ten rowdy children dug up the potatoes. They put them into sacks to sell to grocery stores.

*Did the skinny man find the arrowhead?*

No. Times were hard, and the skinny man ran out of money. He and his round wife and his ten rowdy children moved away to the city. The skinny man found a better job.

He sold the land to a farmer with a shiny steel combine and a lot of modern ideas. The farmer planted soybeans in the potato field.

Every year he harvested the soybeans with his shiny steel combine. He sold them to a factory to make chicken feed.

*Did the farmer find the arrowhead?*

No. The farmer's hair turned gray, and his bones started to ache. He decided to retire. He sold the land to the family of a boy named Ted. Ted had wide brown eyes, a big imagination, and a mom and dad who taught him to pray.

Ted's dad planted corn in the soybean field. Sometimes Ted and his big sister Grace and his bigger sister Miriam played hide-and-seek between the stalks of corn.

*Did they find the arrowhead?*

No. But Miriam found another arrowhead down by the creek. And Grace found two, one at the edge of the woods and one in the gravel pit by the old red barn.

Ted wished he could find an arrowhead.
Every night he prayed that he would.

He looked beside the creek and
at the edge of the woods.

He looked in the gravel pit
by the old red barn, but he
couldn't find an arrowhead.

"God can do anything,"
Ted's mom said.

"God answers prayer," said Ted's dad.
Ted wondered if it were true. So far,
God hadn't helped him find an arrowhead.

“Do you think God cares about an arrowhead?” Miriam asked. “Maybe you should pray for the missionaries.”

"Pray for the poor people who need food," said Grace. "You don't really need an arrowhead."

*So did Ted stop praying for an arrowhead?*

No. He didn't stop. He prayed for the missionaries, and he prayed for the poor people, and he prayed for an arrowhead too.

One day his dad was out plowing the field, and his mom said, "Ted, go find your dad and tell him to come in for dinner."

Ted ran over the soft plowed dirt toward his dad on the tractor.
He thought about finding an arrowhead,
and he prayed a little prayer as he ran.

"Dear God, *(Step, step)*

help me *(Step, step)*

to find *(Step, step)*

an arrowhead."

Then Ted looked down,
and what do you think he saw?

*What? What did he see?*

He saw the arrowhead, lying on top of the dirt the plow had turned up. It was wide, wider than Miriam's and wider than Grace's. He could see the chisel marks where the Indian had carved it from stone.

*What did he do?*

He picked up the arrowhead and ran across the soft plowed dirt toward his dad. The arrowhead felt smooth and sharp curled up in his palm. He prayed another prayer as he ran. It went like this:

"Thank You, God *(Step, step)*

for the arrowhead." *(Step, step)*

*(Step, step)*

Then he showed it to his dad, and they both went in for dinner.

*Is that the end?*

Yes, that's the end.

*Can I see the arrowhead?*

Yes, you can see it. Here it is.

# A Brief Timeline of the Arrowhead's History

**Early 1800s and prior:** Native Americans from Iroquois and Algonquian nations lived in Indiana, "Land of the Indians." A major battle between these two groups took place near where my dad grew up in Wakarusa, Indiana. The arrowhead he found could have been shot during battle, but instead, I picture it as being shot by an Indian hunting food for his family.

**1840-1929:** During the 1840s, most of the Indians were encouraged or forced to move out of Indiana. Thousands of white settlers hewed farms from the dense forests, and Indiana became a hub of industry. The industrious Hoosier population jumped from a few thousand in 1800 to almost 1½ million in 1860. It is during this era that I picture the first settlers clearing the land and then their son taking over to modernize the farm.

**1929-1941:** These are the years of the Great Depression, and my imagined potato farmer has the misfortune to buy land right at the beginning of it. A few years into the '30s, he and his round wife and his ten rowdy children are forced to move on.

**1941-1960:** In the 1940s, due in part to increased demand brought on by World War II, soybean farming in America boomed. Also in this era, the push toward modern farming continued, with new machinery making the farmer's job ever easier and more efficient. It is here that my enterprising soybean farmer finds his niche.

**1960s-Present:** My dad still has the arrowhead he found as a boy, and he shows it to his children and grandchildren.

Christian Light Publications is a nonprofit, conservative Mennonite publishing company providing Christ-centered, Biblical literature including books, Gospel tracts, Sunday school materials, summer Bible school materials, and a full curriculum for Christian day schools and homeschools. Though produced primarily in English, some books, tracts, and school materials are also available in Spanish. For more information about the ministry of CLP or its publications, or for spiritual help, please contact us at:


CHRISTIAN LIGHT PUBLICATIONS
P. O. Box 1212
Harrisonburg, VA 22803-1212

Telephone: 540-434-0768
Fax: 540-433-8896
E-mail: info@clp.org
Website: www.clp.org